GRAPHIC BIOGRAPHIES

WILMA RUDOLPH
Olympic Track Star

by Lee Engfer

illustrated by Cynthia Martin
and Anne Timmons

Consultant:
Billie Luisi-Potts, Executive Director
National Women's Hall of Fame
Seneca Falls, New York

Capstone
press

Mankato, Minnesota

Graphic Library is published by Capstone Press,
151 Good Counsel Drive, P.O. Box 669, Mankato, Minnesota 56002.
www.capstonepress.com

1 2 3 4 5 6 11 10 09 08 07 06

Library of Congress Cataloging-in-Publication Data
Engfer, Lee, 1963–
    Wilma Rudolph: olympic track star / by Lee Engfer; illustrated by Cynthia Martin and
Anne Timmons.
        p. cm.—(Graphic library. Graphic biographies)
    Includes bibliographical references and index.
    ISBN-13: 978-0-7368-5489-4
    ISBN-10: 0-7368-5489-4
    1. Rudolph, Wilma, 1940– —Juvenile literature. 2. Runners (Sports)—United States—
Biography—Juvenile literature. 3. Women runners—United States—Biography—Juvenile
literature. I. Martin, Cynthia. II. Timmons, Anne. III. Title. IV. Series.
GV1061.15.R83E54 2006
796.42'092—dc22   2005024500

Summary: In graphic novel format, tells the life story of Wilma Rudolph, hero of the 1960 Rome
    Olympics.

Art Director
Jason Knudson

Designer
Bob Lentz

Storyboard Artist
Bob Lentz

Production Artist
Alison Thiele

Colorist
Cynthia Martin

Editor
Tom Adamson

Editor's note: Direct quotations from primary sources are indicated by a yellow background.

Direct quotations appear on the following pages:
Pages 8, 10, 13, 14 (Mae's 2nd line), 17, 18, 22, 24, 25, from *Wilma* by Wilma Rudolph (New
    York: New American Library, 1977).
Page 14 (Mae's 1st line), from *Wilma Rudolph* (VHS) by Andrew Schlessinger (Bala Cynwyd,
    Penn.: Schlessinger Media, 1995).

TABLE OF CONTENTS

Page

Chapter

1   The Sickly Kid   4

2   The Runner   10

3   The 1960 Olympics in Rome   16

4   An Inspiration to Others   24

More about Wilma Rudolph 28
Glossary 30
Internet Sites 30
Read More 31
Bibliography 31
Index 32

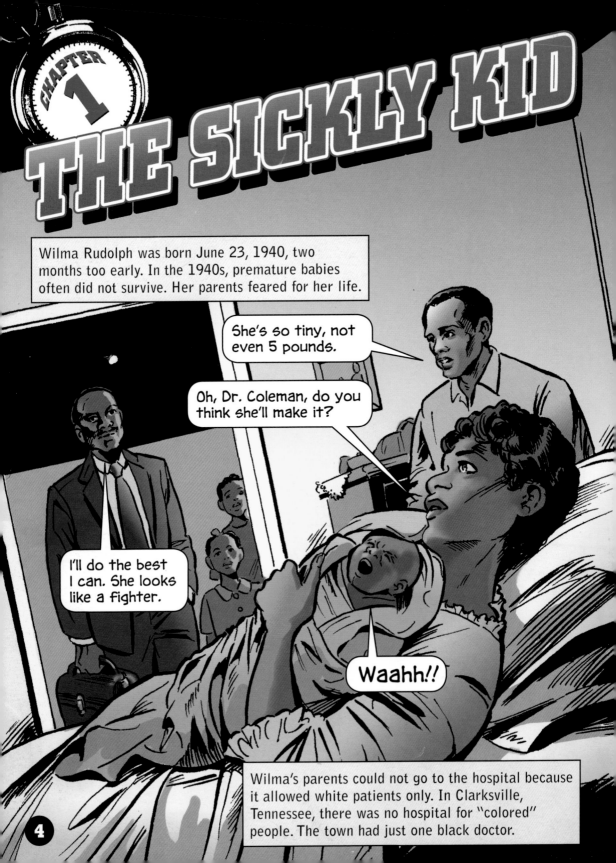

CHAPTER 2 THE RUNNER

In the fall of 1952, 12-year-old Wilma entered 7th grade at Burt High School. Students in grades 7 through 12 went to this all-black school.

Wilma showed up early for every basketball practice and worked hard. But Coach Clinton Gray wouldn't put her in a game.

Coach Gray, how come I'm not playing?

You're buzzing around like a skeeter wherever I turn!

From then on, she had a new nickname, Skeeter.

Keep practicing. Your time will come.

Finally, when Wilma was in 10th grade, Coach Gray chose her as one of the players to start in the games. Wilma was a top scorer.

She was also good at stealing the ball from the other team.

The Burt High School girls' basketball team was good enough to make it to the Tennessee state championships in 1956.

That girl is quick. A natural athlete.

Hey, Coach Temple. Bet you could use that girl on your track team at Tennessee State.

That's what I was thinking.

After basketball season, Wilma joined the track team to keep in shape. She won most of her races. She entered her first large track meet in 1956. The best athletes in the South were competing at this meet in Alabama.

Wilma didn't win any of her races.

I thought I was fast. I have a lot of work ahead of me if I want to win against the best runners.

People in Wilma's hometown were thrilled that she was going to the Olympics. Some Clarksville store owners knew that her family did not have much money.

Get whatever you need. We'll take care of everything.

Thank you so much.

Wilma and the rest of the team arrived in Melbourne, Australia, in October 1956. Wilma ran in the 400-meter relay race. During this relay, four racers each run 100 meters.

The U.S. team was not expected to do well. But they placed third.

I'm going for the gold in the next Olympics!

CHAPTER 3

THE 1960 OLYMPICS IN ROME

After the 1956 Olympics, Wilma went back to life as a high school student. She graduated in June 1958. That fall she entered Tennessee State University.

Wilma continued to train with Coach Temple's track team. In 1960, the team traveled to Texas for the Olympic tryouts.

This can't be right! Something must be wrong with this watch.

Wilma's first event was the 100-meter dash. She took first place in the race, winning the gold medal.

Her next race was the 200-meter dash. She knew there was nobody alive who could beat her in that race.

That's two gold medals down and one to go.

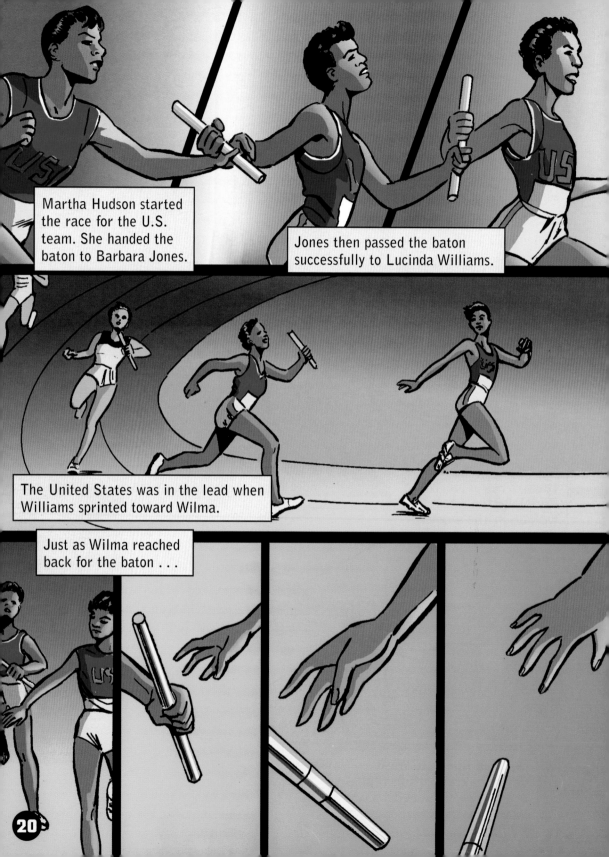

Martha Hudson started the race for the U.S. team. She handed the baton to Barbara Jones.

Jones then passed the baton successfully to Lucinda Williams.

The United States was in the lead when Williams sprinted toward Wilma.

Just as Wilma reached back for the baton . . .

Back in the United States, Wilma received a hero's welcome. Many cities held parades. But the best one was in her hometown.

Later, the town held a dinner for Wilma.

To Wilma!

Black and white people celebrating together in Clarksville, Tennessee! That's as much a victory as winning a gold medal.

It was the first public event in Clarksville to include both white and black citizens. In fact, Wilma wouldn't attend if it turned out to be a segregated event.

23

CHAPTER 4

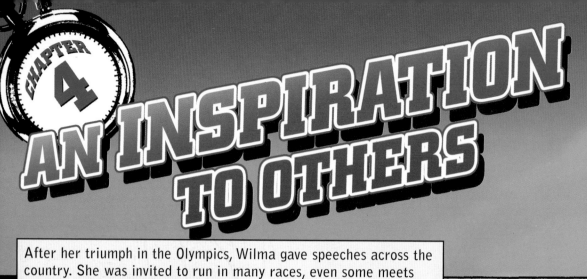

AN INSPIRATION TO OTHERS

After her triumph in the Olympics, Wilma gave speeches across the country. She was invited to run in many races, even some meets that were for men only. Then she went back to finish college.

By the end of 1961, Wilma was trying to decide if she should try for a third Olympics.

Now what should I do? I know I can't run forever.

To go back to the Olympics in 1964 and lose will diminish everything you've already accomplished.

More about WILMA RUDOLPH

Wilma Glodean Rudolph was born June 23, 1940.

Wilma had 21 brothers and sisters. Her father, Ed Rudolph, had 14 children in his first marriage. After he married Blanche, the couple had eight more children.

In the 1940s, polio struck thousands of children each year. Polio is a virus that spreads just like a cold. The disease causes fever, fatigue, vomiting, and pain in the limbs. One out of every 200 people who got polio became paralyzed. By 1954, polio had killed or crippled more than 350,000 Americans. There is no cure for polio, but a vaccine was invented in 1954, which prevents the disease.

In 1947, when Wilma started school, black and white students in the South had to go to different schools. States usually gave less money to African American schools. These schools got by with fewer teachers. They had older buildings, books, and equipment. In the 1950s, the U.S. Supreme Court ruled that segregated black schools were not equal to white schools.

In a tour of Europe after the 1960 Olympics, fans went crazy for Wilma. In Cologne, Germany, police had to hold back the crowd. In Berlin, fans surrounded her bus and beat on it with their fists until she waved.

Wilma and her husband, Robert Eldridge, had four children: Yolanda, Djuana, Robert, and Xurry.

In 1977, Wilma wrote a book about her life. The book, *Wilma*, was made into a TV movie starring Cicely Tyson and Denzel Washington.

In 1980, Tennessee State University named its indoor track for Wilma Rudolph. That year she was also named to the Women's Sports Hall of Fame.

In 1994, Wilma was diagnosed with brain and throat cancer. She died November 12, 1994. She was just 54 years old.

GLOSSARY

autograph (AW-tuh-graf)—a person's handwritten signature

dash (DASH)—a short race

determination (de-tur-min-AY-shuhn)—making a decision to accomplish something and not changing your mind

massage (muh-SAHZH)—to rub with the fingers and hands to loosen muscles or to help a person relax

paralyzed (PAIR-uh-lyzed)—unable to move or feel a part of the body

premature (pree-muh-TOOR)—too early

relay (REE-lay)—a race involving a team; each team member covers part of the race. In a 400-meter relay, each runner covers 100 meters.

retire (ri-TIRE)—to give up a line of work

segregated (SEG-ruh-gate-ed)—separated, or forced apart; racial segregation is separation by race.

sprint (SPRINT)—to run fast for a short distance

tryout (TRYE-out)—a test to see if a person is qualified to do something

INTERNET SITES

FactHound offers a safe, fun way to find Internet sites related to this book. All of the sites on FactHound have been researched by our staff.

Here's how:

1. Visit *www.facthound.com*
2. Type in this special code **0736854894** for age-appropriate sites. Or enter a search word related to this book for a more general search.
3. Click on the **Fetch It** button.

FactHound will fetch the best sites for you!

READ MORE

George, Charles. *Life under the Jim Crow Laws.* The Way People Live. San Diego: Lucent Books, 2000.

Krull, Kathleen. *Wilma Unlimited: How Wilma Rudolph Became the World's Fastest Woman.* San Diego: Harcourt, 1996.

Naden, Corinne J., and Rose Blue. *Wilma Rudolph.* African-American Biographies. Chicago: Raintree, 2004.

Ruth, Amy. *Wilma Rudolph.* Minneapolis: Lerner, 2000.

Schraff, Anne E. *Wilma Rudolph: The Greatest Woman Sprinter in History.* African-American Biographies. Berkeley Heights, N.J.: Enslow, 2004.

BIBLIOGRAPHY

Biracree, Tom. *Wilma Rudolph.* American Women of Achievement. New York: Chelsea House, 1988.

Roberts, M.B. "Rudolph Ran and World Went Wild." ESPN.com. http://espn.go.com/sportscentury/features/00016444.html.

Rudolph, Wilma. *Wilma.* New York: New American Library, 1977.

Schlessinger, Andrew. *Wilma Rudolph.* VHS. American Women of Achievement Video Collection. Bala Cynwyd, Penn.: Schlessinger Media, 1995.

INDEX

Burt High School, 10, 12

Clarksville, Tennessee, 4, 6, 15, 23
Coleman, Dr., 4, 8

Eldridge, Robert (husband), 25, 29

Faggs, Mae, 14

Gray, Coach Clinton, 10–11

Meharry Medical College, 6
Melbourne, Australia, 15

Nashville, Tennessee, 6, 7, 9

Olympic Games
    1956, 15
    1960, 17, 18–22, 29
Olympic Trials, 14, 16–17
Operation Champ, 26

polio, 6, 28

Rome, Italy, 17
Rudolph, Blanche (mother), 4–9, 13, 28

Rudolph, Ed (father), 4–5, 13, 28
Rudolph, Wilma
    birth of, 4, 28
    childhood of, 5–9
    children of, 25, 29
    death of, 29
    illnesses of, 5, 6, 8
    and leg brace, 6, 8, 9
    and Olympic medals, 15, 18–19, 22
    retirement of, 25
    and school, 7, 8, 10, 12, 16
    speeches of, 24, 27
    and sports, 10–13

segregation, 4, 7, 23, 28

Temple, Coach Ed, 12–14, 16, 24
Tennessee State University, 12, 13, 16, 24–25, 29

Wilma Rudolph Foundation, 27